HOLDING
EVERYTHING
DOWN

Crab Orchard Series in Poetry
First Book Award

Holding
Everything
Down

WILLIAM
NOTTER

Crab Orchard Review
&
Southern Illinois
University Press
Carbondale

The Crab Orchard Series in Poetry is a joint publishing venture of Southern Illinois University Press
and *Crab Orchard Review.* This series has been made possible by the generous support of the Office
of the President of Southern Illinois University and the Office of the Vice Chancellor for Academic
Affairs and Provost at Southern Illinois University Carbondale.

Crab Orchard Series in Poetry Editor: Jon Tribble
First Book Award Judge for 2008: Ricardo Pau-Llosa

"Me and Bobby McGee" words and music by Kris Kristofferson and Fred Foster. Copyright
© 1969 (renewed 1997) Temi Combine Inc. All rights controlled by Combine Music Corp. and
administered by EMI Blackwood Music Inc. All rights reserved. International copyright secured.
Used by permission.

Library of Congress Cataloging-in-Publication Data
Notter, William, date,
  Holding everything down / William Notter.
     p. cm. — (Crab Orchard series in poetry)
  ISBN-13: 978-0-8093-2927-4 (alk. paper)
  ISBN-10: 0-8093-2927-1 (alk. paper)
  I. Title.
  PS3614.O79H65 2009
  811'.6—dc22   2009007804

for Tara

CONTENTS

ACKNOWLEDGMENTS

Grateful acknowledgment is made to the following publications, where some of these poems first appeared (sometimes in slightly different versions):

AGNI Online—"Jubilate"

Alaska Quarterly Review—"The Dead Guy Clears the Air about Roadkill"

Alligator Juniper—"Have You Seen Anna?"

Ascent—"The Big Horn Range"

Chattahoochee Review—"First Love" and "The Trailer House on Bethel Road"

The Chester H. Jones Foundation National Poetry Competition Winners, 1999— "Directions in the Nebraska Sandhills"

Connecticut Review—"At the Washita River Battle Site"

Crab Orchard Review—"The Dead Guy and the Evangelist," "Greatest of These Is Fire," "Slow Progress on Chickasaw Ridge," and "Wyoming Highways"

High Desert Journal—"Above Medicine Mountain" and "Postcard"

The Midwest Quarterly—"Grandview Point"

Poet Lore—"Demolition Derby"

Southern Poetry Review—"Accused," "Heavy Metal Frontman," and "Personnel Orientation"

Willow Springs—"Worship"

The Yalobusha Review—"The View from Woodall Mountain, Elevation 806"

Some poems first appeared in the chapbook *More Space Than Anyone Can Stand*, published by Texas Review Press (2002). Many thanks to Paul Ruffin.

"High Plains Farming" was reprinted in *Good Poems for Hard Times*, edited by Garrison Keillor (Viking, 2005).

"Gray's First Sober Year," "High Plains Farming," and "Morning News in the Big Horn Mountains" were broadcast on *The Writer's Almanac* from American Public Media.

Thanks to the Nevada Arts Council, Sierra Arts Foundation, and the Walton Family Foundation for grants and fellowships that helped me complete this book.

For their insight and support, I am grateful to the late James Whitehead, Miller Williams, Jon Tribble, Enid Shomer, Ricardo Pau-Llosa, Margaret McMullan, Davis McCombs, Michael Heffernan, Mike Carson, Bill Baer, the Friday night barbecue regulars, Cathy Hunter, and, especially and always, Tara Bray.

ONE

Rusty the Finisher

Rusty was looking for a trowel in the cab of his truck
when he pulled out the urn. Brass, engraved with leaves,
his mother, he says. He can finish a slab so smooth
it shines when it's dried. *Why in your truck?* I ask.
She was born by the ocean, in Oregon.
She wants to be dumped out there.
He shakes the urn and it clinks like pebbles
in a concrete truck. *I hear that sound sometimes*
when I'm driving. Rusty's never seen the ocean.
Three years he's been too busy for a trip to Oregon.
Always concrete jobs, highways
or foundations to pour, then rodeos
on the weekends. *Don't they have bucking horses*
and mud to finish on the coast? I say.
He sets the urn behind the pickup seat.
If he dumped her in the river, she'd run to the Mississippi
and then to the Gulf. *Wrong ocean,* he says.
It wouldn't be right. I need to do things
the way she wants this time. Come on,
mud's on the way. We've got forms to set.

Wheat Harvest

I have a girl who will lie with me
to watch purple flaring thunderheads,
a Chevy to hotrod on Sundays off,
all the overtime I can stand
at the farmers' co-op tire shop.
Daylight sinks each evening
into fields beyond the edge of town.
Wheat trucks line up at the scales,
dust swirling in the running lights.
The darkness quiets July's dry wind,
and carries the smell of grain in from the plains.

Air from the impact gun blows hot,
busting truck tires hot from the road
on these blazing days at the shop.
Trucks come in with retreads flapping,
sidewalls blown, shredded tubes.
I patch and bang and pry all day
on the semi radials, the split-rings,
the rusty widowmaker wheels.
They're always rushing to get back,
roaring toward the field, the next load,
empty trailers banging through the ruts
they've gouged in Main Street's tar.

Before long those harvest crews
will haul their combines through the dark,
threshing a path to Canada.
They will stop where daybreak spreads

across a bristling ripe horizon,

heads of grain as far as anyone can see

nodding in the sideways light.

They will leave behind stubble,

tire carcasses, chaff in the streets,

my nagging dreams about the way they move.

The Ranch Woman's Secret

Arlan thinks I'm here to watch the sunset
the days he finds me still outside on the deck.
It would likely be grounds for divorce if he knew,
but I'm here listening for coyotes who cry in the hills
when the sun is gone and twilight purples the east.
I do the books, and I know he's wasted more
on traps and shells and bait than we've ever lost
to coyotes. We haven't had a single head
killed by anything but cold and blizzards
or the scours in years. I know it's the bank note
and the markets he mumbles about while he sleeps,
but it's coyotes in the morning. He can't sit still
thinking of all the space they've got to hide in.
And the harder he fights to run them out,
the more I hear wailing in the hills at night.
We saw one crossing the road one evening, her coat
like ruffled wheat, looking back at us
as if we were out of place. Arlan stopped
the truck and shot her with his coyote rifle.
She spun once, biting the wound, then dropped,
and he hung her carcass on the barbed wire fence.
I fell asleep on the couch every night that week,
but he never knew why. He'll start to wonder
where he put his seven-millimeter shells
and how his traps get sprung while he's in town
or hauling a load of hay from Nebraska. The coyotes
won't let him win, and I'll keep staying out
past dark to listen, to hear the anxious cries
that make these nights, this stubborn life, seem real.

High Plains Farming

There's never enough of the right kind of rain,
and always too much of what we get.
We've got no need for casinos—
keeping the farm is enough to gamble on.
If the seed doesn't blow out of the ground in December,
the wheat gets laid down flat in the fields by hail
come summer. Spring blizzards get the calves,
and one year my corn was nothing
but rows of stalks from softball-size hail
a month before harvest. That storm ruined my roof
and beat siding right off the neighbors' house.

A little hail and wind can't run me off, though,
and I'll keep dropping the well until the aquifer
dries up like they've said it would for years.
We may not know what it's going to leave us with,
but we can see our weather coming.
When those fronts blow across the fields,
trailing dust and rain, we've got time
to get the cars in the shed, and ourselves
into the basement if the clouds are green.

Next morning I go out to see where the dice fell.
Everything's glazed and bright with the dust knocked off
and the sun barely up. The gravel on the roads
is clean-washed pink, and water still hangs
on the fence wires and the pasture grass.
Sometimes I need to call the county
about a washed-out road, or the insurance man

about a field stripped clean. When I'm lucky
I can shut the irrigation pumps down
for a day or two and give the well a rest.

I like to drive right into it sometimes
when a storm comes up, lightning arcing
all directions over the hills, and the slate-blue
edge of the front clean as a section line.
There's an instant in that border
where it's not quite clear but not the storm
when everything seems to stop, like my wheels
have left the road. The light turns spooky, dust
just hangs, grass glows like it's ready
to spark and catch on fire. Then the motor strains,
fat raindrops whack the tin and glass
like the racket from a flock of blackbirds,
hundreds of them scattering off a stubblefield.

Personnel Orientation

She explains the retirement plan,
what the insurance pays
and what it won't. Reviewing
the section on dependent benefits,
it comes out, in different words,
what a deadbeat her ex-husband is.
Her big eyes and the nervous way
she keeps tucking hair behind one ear
make you want to trust her.
At her office, when you return the forms,
she points to a water bowl outside,
to the crow tossing sandwich crusts
and tapping on the window glass.

Accused

We want to be able to say he looks evil,
that he sneers at the television cameras
or chuckles in court like a maniac.
A spatter of the girl's blood is in his car.
Volunteers on the snow-crusted fields
have found nothing but a shoe
in the ditch beside a county road.
He only looks bewildered,
a handyman, getting old, silent
as though in shock from an accident.
Deputies corral him past reporters
with a flak vest over his farmer's coat.

The Dead Guy from Nebraska By-Product

In hot weather, cows will swell in the sun
until their udders go purple and one leg jacks up high.
The truck holds more if I stab the stomachs
and let the bloat go down. Sometimes
the vet's done an autopsy and the stitches break
while I'm winching one in—a pitchfork
is the only way to get around that.
Of course I've seen the two-headed calves
and a few with an extra leg on their sides—
those don't live for long if they're born alive.

The Dead Guy's here! The Dead Guy's here!
that kid at the dairy on Six tells his folks
when I pull in the yard. I don't stop there often,
since the feedlots always have most of the wrecks.
I think of the deads as wrecks—
like a broke-down truck you tow from the shed
on the morning it finally won't start.

That boy watched me winch a bony Swiss
into the box one time. Had a stick with him,
like he wanted to poke her but was scared to.
That's Belinda, he said. *My dad had to shoot her
cause she wouldn't stand up.* Those are the worst—
cows that go down and can't get their feet again.
They've got a sour smell, not just rot
but garlicky, like they sweated hard while they died.
He asked me where I was taking her to,
and I said she'd go to make baloney. His eyes
got big as sunflowers and he didn't say a word.

It's not a bad job. You get used to the smell—

it just smells like cows after awhile.

It's not me stuck in the rendering plant

skinning and cooking down the deads.

I get to see the countryside,

scout good spots to hunt pheasants,

watch the sun coming up in the sandhills.

We keep people's dogs and cats fed—the baloney's a joke.

The vet breeds as many as I haul off,

and there's bulls, and seems like always calves.

The Dead Guy Clears the Air about Roadkill

The Denver talk show station had a lady call
and rave about rendering plants collecting pets—
grinding up cats with hair, flea collars,
little bells and all, making dog food
from people's passed-on dogs.
She said the drivers will even stop
to pick up roadkill deer, coyotes, prairie dogs,
and imagine the diseases that could pass
from kibble to pets to owners.

Now I can't say how they do it
in the city, but I'm paid to pick up cattle—
beef mostly, sometimes dairy—
and every now and then a horse.
A full-grown hog is fine if it's on my route,
but big operations usually bury theirs.
I've hauled away a donkey, and exotics
like one man's ostrich, but left his neighbor's dog
right where he'd shot it going under the fence.

Skunks, raccoons, possums, badgers, and deer
are a job for the county road crew,
trusties from the jail, or coyotes and crows.
I will not pick up a dog or cat for anyone
who needs to bury it or sneak it into the dump himself.
If you see me stopped along the road,
I'll be checking tires or taking a leak,
not peeling bullsnakes off the blacktop
or hunting for smashed-up turtles
to try and add more weight to my load.

How One Thing Led to Another for the Dead Guy

I wound up here because of a barrel racer,
a Wyoming gal with pretty jeans
and a three-can-a-week snuff habit.
Followed her from Cody and Billings
to Cheyenne, Greeley, Colorado Springs
and Ogallala finally. She'd ride a bull
if anybody would let her try,
and I saw her stay on a bucking horse
longer than any cowboy on the program.
I've raced a derby car or two
but never cared much about a horse,
even one that doesn't buck.

I kept her outfit tuned, rubbed her shoulders at night,
so nobody called me wild—nothing like
that hotshot Amarillo bullrider
she introduced me to before his ride.
He'd be going with her to Great Bend,
she said, and I figured he'd be handling
wheel bearings and fan belts from then on, too.
That little monkey climbed on Piledriver,
who threw him just outside the chute
and kicked him, too, before he hit the ground.
When the bull went after the clowns,
Amarillo came up with a skinning knife
and cut his throat clean through.

The whole arena stood there stunned
with Piledriver bleeding into the dirt—
clowns, crowd, riders waiting on the fence.
Amarillo had shut things down so long
that I finally drove my pickup through
a side gate and pulled the bull out
with a tow chain looped around his horns.
Before I had the chain undone, the man
who runs the rendering plant was telling me
I showed some kind of initiative
dragging that bull away
while the rest of them stood around.
He said he'd had to let a driver go
that week, and was I looking for a job?

The Dead Guy and the Evangelist

A guy wearing a tie and a soaking shirt
was handing out religious pamphlets
today at the truckstop, asking everybody
have they been saved from eternal damnation by Christ
our personal lord and savior. I'd just picked up
four deads that were three days gone
from the heat down at Shafer Brothers Feedlot.
My mind was on air conditioning and fueling up
so I could get my load back to the plant.
He came over, wearing enough cologne
to keep a dog away from a dead wagon,
and asked me if I know where I'm going
when I die. A rancher who called me once
to carry off a palomino asked
how I liked the resurrection business,
and so I told that preacher I wasn't sure,
but I work in resurrection too,
and had to get a load to Wauneta before it spoiled.

Who is he to ask me where I'm going
when I die? Me and that preacher and a millionaire
will end up drained and pickled and dressed
in suits, and that's all any of us knows.
What's left is just a carcass the undertaker
powders and buries instead of hauling off
to the rendering plant. We both keep
the dead from piling up. People would know
if somebody wasn't there to keep those cows
from laying around getting ripe where they died.

I don't need to imagine more of a heaven
than the light inside of Five Springs Canyon
afternoons when cutthroats pop the surface
and bite on anything you throw in the water,
or watching pheasants break from a field of cornstalks,
or even having Rhonda call me *Darlin'*
when I stop for lunch at the Conestoga Grill.
I won't say I'm ready. But if I got run over
by a sugar beet truck tonight, I could die knowing
I did some good in life, that I was willing
to do a job not many people would do.

Parchman Farm

These days, instead of picking cotton,
the inmates bag run-over dogs
by the roadside, smoke, lift weights.
Hurricane fence and razor wire
lash the prison's low buildings
to the Delta—floodplain
leveed and stripped of trees.
Miles of bayous and moccasins,
copperheads, redbugs, ticks,
and gators, one guard says,
between here and any town.

A Greyhound idles by the gate,
aluminum the pink of hazy sun.
This is Mississippi—
each released man boards with a Bible,
tells how incarceration
and the Lord done changed his ways.
And at the next stop toward Memphis
you can find Bibles by the busload.

Slow Progress on Chickasaw Ridge

All that Mississippi winter, it seemed,
Eddie and I were pumping orange water
and trying to frame up forms to pour
a retaining wall behind the new apartments.
The hillcut sloughed red mud,
the footing trench was flooded every morning
and skinned with ice.

One morning we're warming our toes
at the kerosene heater as we wait
for the pump to drain the hole.
Eddie built himself a plumb-framed
and tight-sided house on the outskirts,
a neighborhood screened by kudzu vines
where only black folks live. Most houses there
are pieced together with scrap tin, blackjack,
even paper plates, and thinking of downtown's
fine homes and historic oaks,
I ask how things have changed in thirty years.

Eddie had a smart mouth, and got sent
to live with an aunt up North for the worst
of what went on in the sixties.
He remembers an old car his cousin had.
The generator was bad, and the cousin would drive
with headlights off to keep the battery charged.
The battery died anyway, once on a shortcut
through the college campus, where the sheriff
caught them coasting down Sorority Row.

Even a white boy from the High Plains,
where blacks were only on TV shows,
can understand the tension as the sheriff
tossed one end of a log chain
to Eddie's cousin and towed them home.

He says it isn't near as dangerous now
and a man can pretty much just live his life.
By noon the sky begins to spit
the season's only snow. *It snowed the night*
I heard that Dr. King got shot,
says Ed, flurries coming down
as he left a Chicago movie house,
his date whose face he can't recall
holding half a sack of popcorn,
the news drifting quietly through the crowd.

The Crossroads, Mississippi

Three preachers with a bullhorn,
three dark suits and umbrellas
blurring into November drizzle,
harangue sinners from the corner.
They replace each other at the verge
of hoarseness, with new fury
against alcohol, fornication, crack.

One of the women raped last week
was taken from a grocery in daylight,
a child attacked his teacher,
a clerk was killed in a robbery.
Shots last night kept on
while sirens eased through town.

Is this wrong?
Think of buying a pistol
that could knock down bear, imagine
the blue indifference of its heft,
the yank of recoil,
slugs that bloom to jagged stars.
Imagine sitting in the dark, praying
for a strung-out, no-count thief
to break a window, or burst
boldly through the door.

Radio Man

Harley Dover could work on anything electric.
Made Ray's uncle a radio twice as good
from two old broken ones,
and built an AM station from junk
that pirated the Thacker Mountain signal.
The law shut it down when they heard him
advertising Tennessee red wigglers,
tried to lock him up for communist messages.

They say he drove Mrs. Dover crazy.
Doctors wanted to send her down
for electroshock at Whitfield.
Thinking he could save a little money,
he wired her bedspring to a wall socket
and got sent to Whitfield himself.

He fixed a doctor's television
so they sent him home in a week,
said he was smarter than anyone there.
Mrs. Dover was gone, took everything
but the radios. People say he lived on squirrel
until he crashed on the Choctaw bridge
and they had to keep him crippled in a home.
He died an old man just like anybody.
Couldn't even change a light by then.

The View from Woodall Mountain, Elevation 806

The red clay and gravel summit
of Mississippi's highest point
suffers the same litter as below—
cans, plate lunch cartons, broken glass,
concrete blocks from a burned foundation.

But climbing the fire lookout tower
opens distance and sky, diversion
from scarred soil washing away.
Darkening hills hide the clearcuts,
creeper thickets and hardscrabble yards.

Sundown layers the horizon orange,
ozone blue salted with stars,
a splinter of moon. The spindly head
of a loblolly shivers in the breeze.
Then voices, an ambulance call

through the tower's radio relay—
thirty year-old male, his windpipe slashed.
The sky settles down to dark,
lights from the yards and farms below
claim their small circles on the ground.

Morning Break, Barksdale Job

We was redoing this old mansion,
oldest house in town, they say.
Lady who owns it wants to rent out rooms
to rich folks, one-fifty a night,
serve up grits and biscuits in the morning.
We're all out front by the columns,
telling deer stories, watching college girls.
Old Jerry pipes up how he don't know
what they sell in that store across the street,
but it sure does make them girls look good.
Finest woman I ever seen walked in there
week and a half, two weeks ago.
Had on them little black tights
the way they wear. Got damn
she's fine as frog's hair.
Painter starts telling lies again
about the prettiest chick he ever saw.
Workin for Sandefers up there
when they put that library in on campus.
This blonde walks by wearin
one of them short hippie dresses.
Gust of wind catches her,
blows that sumbitch
right up over her head,
and she weren't wearin no bra.
Shows how big they were with his hands,
but we don't fall for much he says.
Jerry, he just stares at his coffee
like he still can't believe how fine.

Painter shows off a raggedy skull tattoo

he's got some boy making over

into a twelve-point buck.

Everybody watches the store

until the boss hollers at us,

Just as well be stealin from me

takin break so long.

We all go back to pounding nails,

hanging rock and double insulation

so rich folks won't hear each other screw.

It's enough to help make lunchtime,

thinking about long legs

stepping out of expensive cars

and foreign four-wheel-drives.

Same way a man can make it to five

thinking about the woods,

the big buck prize at the bait shop,

or maybe a run to them casino boats,

free beers and a chance to make it big.

TWO

Morning News in the Big Horn Mountains

The latest movie star is drunk just out of rehab,
two or three cities had extraordinary killings,
and expensive homes are sliding off the hills
or burning again. There's an energy crisis on,
and peace in the Middle East is close as ever.
In Wyoming, just below timberline,
meteors and lightning storms
keep us entertained at night. Last week,
a squirrel wrecked the mountain bluebirds' nest.
I swatted handfuls of moths in the cabin
and set them on a stump each day,
but the birds would not come back to feed.
It snowed last in June, four inches
the day before the solstice. But summer
is winding down—frost on the grass
this morning when we left the ranger station.
Yellow-bellied marmots are burrowing
under the outhouse vault, and ravens leave the ridges
to gorge on Mormon crickets in the meadows.
Flakes of obsidian and red flint
knapped from arrowheads hundreds of years ago
appear in the trails each day,
and the big fish fossil in the limestone cliff
dissolves a little more with every rain.

Haunting Porcupine Ranger Station

She is not an angry ghost.
And so she must have died a common death,
from fever in her second winter,
or bearing a child for the man who brought her
from the coal-choked East or pestilent South
to Wyoming's paradise of gold and sky
and shrieking wind. He pulled down
their canvas tent when the gold played out,
leaving Bald Mountain City to snow
and pocket gophers, leaving her behind,
like beads of quicksilver gleaming in the creek
downstream from where the miners milled their ore.
Her grave is long-unmarked above the townsite,
in a meadow choked with shooting stars,
forget-me-nots and fireweed.

Spending a hundred winters in these hills
has made her wander for recognition
when the summer crews move in.
She sat on the edge of a ranger's bed
as he dreamed, and talked to him of mules
and lemon drops. She is a pocket
of cold roving the cabin at night
while the woodstove stutters and shakes.
She has rearranged mess kits
and first aid supplies in the fire cache.
The women sometimes wake in the night and find
their lotions and lacy things disturbed.

And when the light in the attic above the barn
seems to have been left burning
accidentally, she is there
among the smells of hay and horse-broken leather,
sitting by the window, that butter-yellow square
against the dark and the crackling stars.

White-Throated Swifts

You'll duck before you see the first
whipping past from behind
like something launched or shot.
They accelerate to specks,
boomerang, chattering,
and dive again.
Fighter jets,
their only payload thrills
to see a creature doing
just as it was meant to do.

Grandview Point

A raven rises from the canyon,
fibers of every feather slashing air.
It calls; its mate calls back
and somersaults in perfect blue.

The canyonlands are like the ceiling
of the sky turned upside down
and piled red with clouds.
Stillness thunders down
against varnished cliffrock,
gorge walls that remember
marshes, ocean, dinosaurs.
Morning's bronze light
raises the spice of pine.
Mountains peaked in snow
hum on three horizons.

An old man died
at the base of a juniper here,
canteen empty, his last
roll of film exposed.
The wet part of him,
sponged into sandstone,
must have surrendered
in those final delirious moments
to the tug of silence,
to the gravity of rivers
coursing far below,

and to the hunger of ravens

that would fill themselves with his body,

then spiral up from the canyon rim.

Cottonwood

Lost in a desert with butterscotch walls,
the couple lay down in moonlight.
Each noticed the other's flesh
beginning to taste like wood.
By morning they were a tree.

Their taproot heaves downward in thirst,
their limbs reach outward
into space they could never fill.
Their leaves clatter in the air,
and every year they pour out swarms of seed
that tickle and enrage the wind.

Waking in West Texas

Sunrise profiles the heaving spine
of the Cornudas Mountains
which I never knew were there
as I slept, in the dark.

The sun breaks between peaks,
its light spills over
the mountain range's violet lip
and floods yucca crowns
on the desert bed
with an unfurling of shadows.

This must be like remembering
the moment of birth,
like watching the earth begin.

Above Medicine Mountain

A Northern Cheyenne came to pray
at the ceremonial circle, so I moved far off
talking history and wildflowers
with a few tourists who climbed into altitude
and the threat of storms that afternoon.

He fastened colored cloth to staffs
around the outer ring of stones. The colors—
red, white, yellow, black—meant whatever they meant.
At the center he stood and, who knows,
prayed maybe what any of us would—
thanks for the chipmunks and grass,
that his mind be clear, his people safe,
that he be more thoughtful of his wife.

I can't say if the red-tailed hawk
in its lazy spiral right above the circle
would have come no matter what. But for a believer,
that must be like looking up in church
to see an angel lounging in the rafters.

The Big Horn Range

Layers of the earth upthrust, fractured,
shoved perpendicular against the sky.
Canyons hollowed by water—Porcupine,
Wagon Box, Lodge Grass Creek—
wind funneling over saddle passes,
battering cliffs that once were ocean floor.
Lodgepole pine on thin air,
deadfall drying, ready to awaken in fire.
Raven croak and midair tumble,
frog-bellow of the nighthawk
pulling up from a dive,
chatter and sizzle of white-throated swifts.
Rainbows and cutthroats
fattening down in the Tongue,
elk bugle and mule deer snort,
moose cropping willow shrubs,
coyotes answering a lone sheepdog.
Bear scat, lion print, clean bones
laid out on open hilltops.
Alpenglow flooding meadows
thick with blue-eyed grass,
fireweed and shooting star.
Ancient trail cairns, lichened and sunk,
tipi rings, chert flakes, prayer bundles
hung in the limbs of wind-savaged firs.
The glacial pull of gravity,
basement rock heaving up,
starlight behind black trees,
quiet, a falling awake, an opening.

Postcard

Smells like mushrooms & horses up
this high. Frost on the tent mornings.
Water from the spring is cold & sweet.
Two days since I've seen a person.
Make you scream like a wildcat
under all these stars. Call when I find
a phone. Back soon.

When he's out in the desert it feels
like she's sharing him with someone else.
He talks about rocks for weeks after,
and she catches him studying his boots
covered in that pink, fine dust,
boots he'll clean just before he leaves
again. Stones appear in his pockets,
and she finds topographic maps
stashed in the cushions like letters.

First Love

A squall of tires in traffic, the solid thump
of a Pontiac eight through dual exhaust
put me back in the Great Black Shark,
its nose like a prow, paint job flaking rust.
But the torque that loud pedal unspooled
could boil tires into second gear,
front end up, carburetor bores
gulping premium and darkness,
riding crossroad connections like waves,
high on the thrill of turning power loose
and holding on. The world tunneled down
to redline hum and blacktop,
motor thrashing in perfect tune,
threading bridges at one thirty-five
underneath a swollen, greasy moon.

The Trailer House on Bethel Road

Lived up here like a bunch of trash,
the landlord said to Kay and me.
Their sorriness was a double insult
just up the hill from his triple-wide
and in the worn-out place he couldn't let go
because it's where his father died.
He showed us what he'd repaired, gas lines
underneath where they tied their dogs,
all-new fixtures for the broken lights,
and whatall that wild kid tore up.

Mattresses that needed burning years ago,
the stink that came with the windows closed,
fist holes in the bedroom doors,
we were broke, and couldn't manage more.
Kay's boy found a clothes dryer
in the woods out back, devil stars
and swastikas gouged into the paint.
Letters hidden on a closet shelf
said things like *go ahead and tell Daddy*
all he can do is whip me again.

Christ knows what happened here
under *Bless This House* in needlepoint,
The Last Supper in a tinwork frame.
Some nights I woke and turned away,
wondering if rage could live on in a house,
kept awake by rattling drafts and ceiling tile
stained the creeping brown of someone else's luck.

Spreading the Word

If the gods were desperate for converts,
religion would work like the feeling
that shivers from your stomach
up the front of your spine,
then flares at the base of your skull
when you've taken as many pulls
as you can from a vodka jug
before you need to stop and breathe.

Communion would feel like that.
First-timers would become believers,
and the faithful would keep coming back,
thinking *I would feel this way forever
if I could get just a little more.*

Heavy Metal Frontman

He was quoted once in a magazine,
Guitar God or *Titanium Thunder,*
saying he didn't want to be on his deathbed
thinking "Damn, I wish I'd nailed that chick."
That was before the band broke up,
before the overdoses, drug charges, DUIs.
He nailed one for sure this time, tossed her
against the wall of her room at a Nevada
bunny ranch. His mugshot face
is swollen with middle age and booze,
who in his day must have had to limit girls
to three or four at the end of every show.
He's come from the plenty of leather-and-stud
rebellion to trailers in the brush, paneled walls,
windows draped in purple lace. Even there
he can't pay enough to take what it is he needs.

Burkett, Cleaning Up

I never knew my bones could hurt so bad.
The nurse told me the good news
that she's never seen anyone killed by withdrawals,
but all the while I'm jerking like a chicken,
wishing I could go ahead and die.
My counselor showed his tracks and flattened veins
to prove he was a junkie once himself.
Detox will give me something to think about
if I consider firing up again, he said.
And even now I remember that first good fix,
like falling into the hands of God.

I've been well enough to sit in therapy group
the last three days. Benny the drunk tells us
a good woman and a job could keep him dry,
and the crystal meth addict talks about a dealer
he owes a thousand bucks and who he thinks
is watching from the trees across the road.
I sit beside a black-haired woman
who moves across a room like a panther,
but I can't quit staring at that crystal freak.
Christ, he has got gorgeous veins.

Breakfast at the Road Runner Cafe

CAFE still burning in neon after sunup,
and a bird's gangly silhouette stretched out
with speed—the sign draws me in.
The walls inside are hung with Spanish prayers,
kachina dolls, chili pepper bundles,
and a three-foot Christ sanctifies relief
from the bluster of New Mexico spring.

The waitress brings coffee and cream.
The gaunt, mustachioed cook
whets his spatula against the grill
scrambling *huevos Mexicanos*
with chopped green chilies, tomatoes, onion,
tortillas and beans on the side.
A whiskered man at the counter brags
to the waitress about the money he can make
selling copper wire for scrap,
and how he drank thirteen beers
the night before, and wasn't even drunk.
Highway patrolmen talk knockdown power
and calibers, a courthouse blown apart
by a fertilizer bomb in the back of a truck.
A skittish Navajo woman, *Drug Free and Proud*
printed on her shirt, opens a letter
and swirls ice cubes with her butter knife.

The letter might be from a son locked up
for stealing cars in Albuquerque,
a power disconnect notice, or news

her sister died of exposure out in the hills.
Maybe she's just back to the world
from a stay in detox, chewing ice
to keep from thinking she could walk downtown
and be served a bottle of gin
or eighth-ounce bag of weed
as easily as eggs and toast.

A stranger can only say so much
in the open noise of sputtering grease,
small talk, spoons clacking in coffee mugs.
If she can just hold tight to something,
those cravings will disappear the way wind
blows mountains of cloud across the sky.
She could find comfort in a place like this,
the silvery riffle of cottonwood leaves outside,
a novena candle flickering by the door
to keep Jesus lit at night, find pleasure
in good food and desert light across the tables.

The woman lays a few bills down
by her plate of half-eaten eggs,
and walks outside to the payphone.
She holds her black hair with one hand
against the lashing wind. What can a stranger say?
The Santa Fe's red and yellow engines
come thrumming west beside the highway
as I go out the door. *Hang on.* She turns
and I shout again, *Just hang on.*
Past the train is sandstone sunbleached yellow,
knobby juniper clutching at the hills.

Gray's First Sober Year

This new life is better
than a dozen beer-joint romances
or a hundred drunks at fishing camp.
My habit now is *not* drinking,
and waking up where I belong.
I can see colors again,
and I don't feel like a turd in the punchbowl
whenever I go around people.

I'll mow the weeds for Sharon
and almost enjoy it. She's even given up
checking my breath whenever I come home.
I went shopping for our anniversary
and wound up crying in the store,
but not the kind of tears you cry
when your wife catches you lying in the shed
with your pistol jabbed up in your mouth
and vodka running out your nose.

The only thing she could think to do
was check me into another detox,
and this time it finally took.
This year has made me somebody different—
vodka never could do that for long.
Some days when I wake up early
and listen to Sharon lying there breathing,
it feels like somebody snuck in while we slept
and changed our sheets.

THREE

Worship

Lightning outside the darkened room
flickers blue against her skin

and little but time has passed since men
kneeled at fires and carved
the figures of their dread and wonder,
idols of abundant women,
and risked their lives in the hunt

for this same astounding warmth
for the same quicksilver flesh.

Roadside Motel

She is different when he awakens.
She faces the window,
wearing only the silver boots
she bought in Amarillo.
She has taken up smoking.

The cafe outside fills with truckers.
A dusting of snow has stuck
in clumps of yucca, and flakes
gust across the interstate
against a row of peaks.

It's unlike her to stand at a window
naked. He enjoys it.
He tries to lay her across the bed
to do what she was too tired for
last night. She says it's late
and they need to get moving.
She watches the mountains and smokes.
Diesels thunder down the grade,
turbochargers wailing.

Tammy at the Cut Above

You should hear the things that people tell me.
Once I get my hands in their hair
they can't shut up. Yesterday
a lady told me she came home
and found her husband dressed in her lingerie.
As soon as she gets her hands into my hair,
she tells me about the hardbody Russian
she started dating after a shampoo and cut.
Two weeks later, when he proposed,
she decided a green card was all he wanted.
Twelve years was long enough—
she's not ready for the wrong man again.
Anyway, married men make passes at her
more than the single ones, she says.
I'm losing what it probably takes to catch
a hairdresser. I say to trim the top
like I would have when I was seventeen,
and she does with a few slow snips.
She's businesslike as she gathers hair,
tilts my head, and clips. Her body
never brushes against me, but I pretend
that sliver of space between us is charged,
let myself imagine a hairdresser wild
for bald-headed men, pretend
she wore those worn-out jeans
because she knew that I'd be in today.
Then, she's undoing and taking off
my cape, brushing hair from my neck,
asking how it looks.

She takes a phone call—the lawyer
she trims every other Tuesday
wants to take her to Acapulco.
She hopes he isn't married.

Greatest of These Is Fire

I drive eighteen hours straight
to sneak under flannel sheets beside her,
warmth I haven't felt in weeks,
and an hour after I kiss her awake she says,
I don't think I love you anymore.
So I turn back to the highway
and cringe at country all horizon,
rangeland where we used to lie
laughing with the cries of coyotes.
Wind pries around the car's windows,
and low-hung winter sun
chaps me raw as the prairie sky.
I almost lose myself
to the blue shoulders of bluffs,
to the road's rhythm through draws
channeled by summer creeks.
The land carries me on
to places I won't imagine yet,
holding the steering wheel
as a cottonwood grips the sand.
In the rearview, near Great Bend,
sunset spreads against the sky like flames
back when the grasses were tall
and wildfire burned the year's old growth away.

Half-Rack at the Rendezvous

She had a truck, red hair,
and freckled knees and took me all the way
to Memphis after work for barbecue.
We moaned and grunted over plates of ribs
and sweet iced tea, even in a room of strangers,
gnawing the hickory char, the slow
smoked meat peeling off the bones,
and finally the bones. We slurped
grease and dry-rub spice from our fingers,
then finished with blackberry cobbler
that stained her lips and tongue.

All the trees were throwing fireworks
of blossom, the air was thick
with pollen and the brand-new smell of leaves.
We drove back roads in the watermelon dusk,
then tangled around each other, delirious
as honeybees working wisteria.
I could blame it all on cinnamon hair,
or the sap rising, the overflow of spring,
but it was those ribs that started everything.

Jubilate

Now I will consider my purple Plymouth Duster.

For it was assembled in Michigan the month of my conception.

For Plum Crazy is the name of its color.

For that color survives only in the door jambs and inside the trunk.

For the exterior paint is dark and cracked and weathering down to
    primer gray.

For its finish proves the car has endured sun and blizzards and hail and
    gravel blown across the plains.

For the roof supports a colony of black mold from five years in the South.

For it has helped me weather the tempests of Colorado, Missouri, three
    women, and Texas.

For it cost me less than some people spend on shoes.

For its starter may be changed without crawling underneath and becoming
    greasy or suffering grime in the eyes.

For its oil filter may be removed from above, without hot oil running
    down the arm.

For its one-barrel carburetor may be overhauled in the kitchen.

For its clutch makes a chattering sound.

For it has three gears which carry it forward and one which carries it back.

For its heater can save the engine from boiling over in traffic on a summer
    day.

For through its vents come the smells of alfalfa, donuts, wheat, cotton
    poison, pine, refinery tar, and the spice of thunderstorms on the
    desert.

For it waits outside restaurants where I eat meat smoked with hickory,
    pecan, or mesquite.

For from beneath its hood comes the oily-hot smell of a Chrysler power-
    plant.

For its front seat becomes comfortable for a tired man of medium height
to lie across.

For there I have lain and looked up at the pulsating stars.

For I have been lulled asleep there by the rustling of cottonwoods and
the running of creeks.

For I have awakened there to find the windows feathered with my frozen
breath.

For I have awakened there to the sun rising over mountains I did not
know existed.

For I have been awakened there by the tapping of dew dripping from
cypress boughs.

For I have awakened there above canyons filled rim-high with fog and
prickly pear.

For I have awakened there to the smell of early sage and the mourning
of doves.

For the car is sturdy and starts promptly and goes and does not hesitate.

For all its mechanisms are manual. It squanders no effort for luxury.

For it has taught me to forget the self through the honest work of hands.

For it lives by an economy of devotion. I maintain it and it carries me.

Passing through Clarksville

Barefoot woman at the burger stand,
sundress and dark, strong calves,
getting into the passenger side of your truck
with the rearend leaking grease—

It's a crime that nobody in your life
will fix your driver's door
and change the differential gasket.
You should have that much at least.

Demolition Derby

Gray skies and the stars and stripes
hang above this rodeo arena
two feet deep with Missouri Ozark mud.
The bombs of our latest war started falling today,
but here, station wagons and giant sedans
bellow and smoke and sling a shrapnel of mud.
We watch from lawn chairs on a rise
between the arena and a railroad line
where freights rumble past and shake the sumac
reddening along the tracks.
This is what we fight for, the announcer says
as the last two cars face off, a dogfight,
each driver aiming to be the last one running.

The Chrysler has avoided crippling hits
in every heat and lunges through the muck
with a race engine snarl. The Number Seven car
is a yellow wreck so mangled
that the make is anybody's guess,
and soon the Chrysler plows that yellow hood
up into the driver's line of sight.
But Seven charges forward, back and forward,
throwing his heap against an opponent
who has him outmuscled and blind.

He lurches against the Chrysler, hissing
sugary coolant, crankshaft bearings knocking,
fan sparking against the radiator,
but out to show what he can do

with tools and junk, the skin of his knuckles,

a month of Sundays and a little bit of nerve.

This is what we fight for.

The spectators are up, shouting,

or shaking their heads as they would

at having to put an old bull down,

and the Chrysler deals a final running blow

that leaves the Seven car stalled and smoking.

California Pasture

Black Angus grazing wheat-blond grass,
a stock tank, windmill turning
against the sky, like any Western range,
except this pasture drops off at an ocean.
Are a California cow's desires
the same as one from Kansas or Wyoming?
Does it dream of bellying into the surf
instead of escaping to a county road?
Does it rest its dewlap on the top strand
of the fence and lust for stacks of kelp
as landlocked cattle fantasize downwind
from circles of sweet, first-cutting hay?
The seaside cows could lick the air for salt.
Their steaks must flake away from the bone.

At the Washita River Battle Site

Oklahoma wind is the only sound today,
unlike the morning Black Kettle's band
was jarred into a frosted dawn by Custer's buglers,
bullets whizzing, hooves crashing through
the creek's brittle skin. The Seventh Cavalry
beat the Cheyenne with surprise that day.
Black Kettle, finished making peace,
fell defending the village. This must have been
as good as any place to die, sheltered
among the river bottom cottonwoods,
buttes blue from distance on the benchlands
where buffalo fed on the yellow-cured grass,
and the sky holding everything down.

The smell of the dead, of burning tipi skins
and eight hundred gutshot horses is gone.
Hereford cattle graze the hillsides now.
Beer cans left by kids on Saturday night
scatter the lawn around three picnic tables,
and the asphalt glitters with broken glass.
The bottom has been cleared and plowed—
red furrows lined with winter wheat,
stretching to the edges of the sky.

Wyoming Highways

Most of the traffic is pickup trucks
caked in bentonite from the methane roads,
or one-ton flatbeds with dually axles
and blue heelers balancing on the back.
But the blacktop slicing through rabbit brush flats
and weather the color of heated steel is perfect
for opening up a highway-geared American car
from the days of cubic inches and metal.
You could wind that Detroit iron up
to a sweet spot well above the posted limit,
where torque will casually pull the grades.
The car would rock on the springs, and growl
from deep in the carburetor throat
yanked wide open, gobbling down pure light.

Bandera County after a Storm

Driving Texas Hill Country, flash flood gauge
at every dip in the road, limestone bluffs
above the Sabinal, deer weaving through thickets
of prickly pear, Kris Kristofferson
on the Uvalde station, grumbling *freedom's*
just another word for nothin' left to lose.

The sluicing of tires on a rain-dark road,
Kristofferson's voice rough as the crumbling hills,
a love three states away, gone for good,
and no place at all to be
in a sturdy car sloughing off its paint—
one of those moments, maybe three minutes,
when life is perfect and sad and a song is true.

Have You Seen Anna?

I see the first flyer on a message board
in Wheatland. They are everywhere after that, blue,
yellow, pink, all with your smiling face.
Last seen jogging the mountain loop near Lander,
five-foot-six, one-twelve, blonde. Cash
for information, your family desperate with hope.

I imagine you, twenty-two, hopeful,
waiting on a bench at the station, ready to board
a gone-bound bus. With your bank accounts all cashed,
you left that dusty, one-horse town, blew
that popstand for good. Who knows where you landed—
the West Coast maybe, someplace with an ocean of faces.

The townspeople talk of tragedy, can't face
thoughts of deliberate disappearance. Instead, they hope.
The able-bodied citizens of Lander
have scoured the canyon along the Shoshoni border,
suggesting you slipped. They remember you as a blue-
eyed rodeo queen, as the bank's liveliest cashier.

Out hiking, you stumbled onto a bear's cache,
a fresh deer. You glimpsed a shaggy face,
a mound of muscle reared against the blue
of spruce. Fighting, jabbing at its eyes was hopeless,
it splintered you like a thin pine board.
Your body will grow columbines, you're part of the land.

Or it happened like this—You were drawn by all that land,
the wilderness west of town. With gear secretly cached
you went for the hills, escaping the life that bored
you. Now your home is Mount Washakie's face.
Your folks, and the rancher's son they loved, lost hope
but they'll always remember your eyes when the mountains go blue.

Maybe you met the perfect man at the Bluestem
Club. He travels, photographing landscapes,
camping by streams in his truck. Your parents hoped
you'd settle down with Travis, heir to the Cash
Creek Ranch—a pedigreed life you couldn't face.
You're headed for Alaska, bare feet propped on the dashboard.

We hope against the truth—a van slows, you're pulled aboard.
Our hearts blue like steel toward a man we'll never catch.
An impartial patch of land holds you. We have pictures of your face.

Directions in the Nebraska Sandhills

In the wind-flaked town of Lakeside,
I find two boys with a bow and arrows
shooting at starlings in the elms.
When I ask if the Lodgepole road is paved,
they stare as if I'd spoken Spanish.
But the short one cocks his tractor cap
and says the road is all caliche,
that I'd better go through Alliance.

With long hair and a ramshackle car
I must look like the drug-fiend crazies
their parents tell them about.
I want to tell them how lucky they are
to live in Nebraska's emptiest county.
Ahead of them are shotguns, pheasant,
deer from groves along the Platte.
Then clumsiness with girls, the monotony
of tractors, raking hay. They will hate Lakeside.
They will buy a pickup or souped-up car,
rumble off to Rapid City, Denver, anywhere.

When they find a place without wind
the air will feel like dirty clothes.
They will find country filled with trees,
but dream horizons. They will miss
the smell of alfalfa glistening at dawn.
In mountains they will wish for sunset
the way it looks past Alliance, nothing
but orange sky over all their families work for,

ponds like sheets of Depression glass,
trill of a fencepost meadowlark,
Angus in silhouette, more space
than anyone can stand until he leaves.

Route 66, Arizona, 1953

photograph by Andreas Feininger

The town could be Seligman, Truxton, Holbrook,
nowhere anyone stays for long—a motel,
two garages, a stop on the way to the coast.
The Texaco attendant steps outside
and watches the clouds—will they pass dry today
or finally make good their promise of rain?
Feininger parks his coupe on the gravel shoulder
by the hamburger stand. He sets his camera up
across the road, stops the aperture down
for depth of field, and waits.

A car comes grinding up the rise from the east,
a chrome-spangled Buick squinting in the sun.
A man squatting in the shade beside the gas pump,
who's been spitting and watching the horizon for cars,
adjusts his dungarees and thumbs a ride.
Feininger sets his milkshake down in the weeds,
checks his focus, breathes, and captures
this exposure just as the Buick nears the hitcher.

The hitchhiker now stands frozen, his right thumb out.
A stroke of luck might have taken him to Vegas,
or all the way to the coast. Maybe the Buick
passed, suspicious, sending him back
for cover from the desert sun. It is clear
only that this man, this town, this time

are fixed in the emulsion of memory, stopped
on the brink of change that drives ahead so surely
nobody sees it's come until it's passed.

But the afternoon town with its cars and garages, the man
dreaming of work and a girl in California,
occupy only a third of Feininger's frame.
The rest is the sky that has always drawn us—
Apaches, gold seekers, brokendown Midwest farmers—
sky that can let us believe there still is freedom,
space where we can lose ourselves, another chance
just one day's journey down the road,
a sky piled with springtime clouds
huge and promising as continents.

NOTES

"Grandview Point": The story of finding the real man under the juniper is told in Edward Abbey's *Desert Solitaire*.

"Greatest of These Is Fire": The title comes from a line in William Least Heat-Moon's *PrairyErth*: "The four horsemen of the prairie are tornado, locust, drought, and fire, and the greatest of these is fire, a rider with two faces because for everything taken it makes a return in equal measure." (Houghton Mifflin, 1991, p. 77)

"Jubilate": Thanks (or perhaps apologies) to David Lee. His Christopher Smart–inspired poem about a sow, "Jubilate Agno," inspired this one about a car.

"At the Washita River Battle Site": The idea that Black Kettle was defending his village is based on the accounts from Ralph K. Andrist's *The Long Death: The Last Days of the Plains Indians* and Dee Brown's *Bury My Heart at Wounded Knee*. Other accounts suggest he was shot in the back while fleeing.

"Directions in the Nebraska Sandhills": Caliche is a light-colored layer of hardpan soil common in parts of the High Plains and other semiarid regions.

Other Books in the Crab Orchard Series in Poetry